FAITH & INSPIRATION

BOOK OF PRAYERS & AFFIRMATIONS

WRITTEN BY TOMEKA ARTHUR

COPYRIGHT © 2021 TH PUBLISHING COMPANY
ISBN 978-1-7348911-2-6
ALL RIGHTS RESERVED.
WRITTEN BY TOMEKA ARTHUR

My collection of Inspirational books are based on learning, teachings, and experiences that I have received through His Word. Based on books of the Bible and by the preaching of his Holy Spirit coupled together. I Thank the Lord for enlightening me over the years and helping me to fulfill Jesus will in my purpose of spreading the Word. All the glory belongs to God, give glory unto the Lord and worship him in the beauty of Holiness. The word of God is discipline for us a sheep needs a shepherd Psalms 23 author unknown

Learning that we should always
Fast and Pray
Prayer is communion between an individual and God, a petition to God on behalf of our earthly and spiritual nature.
Prayer is to communicate with God at anytime in your own way being of a humble,
sincere and pure heart.
Fasting is an act of humbleness and a way we can think clearly and focus on God.
Fasting brings clarity, discernment and understanding.
It allows us to understand that we must be truly dependent on God in all things, choosing what

God wants rather than what we want; which is to be closer to him.

Praying and fasting brings us into a close communion with God, we find what God's will is always for our good, our total dependence and trust in him.

I must pray to God for what I want and speak to him with expectancy that it is already done I receive it (the desires of our hearts).

Always know that a God listens and answers.

We are to pray without ceasing.
Praying unselfishly, praying for others.
Helping others to grow in the Lord to prosper in their daily lives to the glory of God. To be in good health, strength and of a sound mind. Praying for others also brings a breakthrough in our own lives, we are servants of the Lord and we all have been placed here on earth to help others. Share in the good news, sharing the miraculous and supernatural stories that happens in our lives and how God has brought us through so many times.

We should always pray be devoted to praying asking for help and making petitions
In daily activities, life journeys, trials, tribulations, and in happiness, we must pray.
Help me to put you first
Help me to seek you first in all things
Help me to obey what you require of me
Help me to allow you to know my priorities and to fulfill your will
Help me to continue to go to church and read my bible, tithe and offerings and outreach
Help me to keep my relationship with you
Help Me to allow you to lead and guide me
Help me to recognize my ways and change them to be like you and remove everything that is not like you
Help me to continue to pray for my enemies and those who sin against me and all others

We must also remember Matthew 6 of the Bible, the "Lord's Prayer" as it is God's word that we have memorized like Psalms 23 and it becomes repetitive. We must not forget that it is the divine order and manner that God wants us to pray in. The things that he has promised to supply us with. Not for what we want for personal gain; but a petition for the things that we need to fulfill his will and purpose as his people who trust and believe.

Ask God for a spirit of hearing, listening, and giving
Pray for a spirit of expectations
Expect to be blessed
Expect to have eternal life
Expect to learn the word and have God write it on our hearts
Expect to work in the house of the Lord
Expect to teach inside and outside of the church
Expect to grow the church and ministry
Expect to love, live, and act as Jesus did
Expect to turn away from your wicked ways
Expect to put God first
Expect to have financial wealth and a full life of prosperity
Expect to grow

Lord protect my eyes, my feet, my soul and my mind so that I can allow you to come through me in whatever you shall have me to do
Let your will be done in my life allow me to use my gifts Lord
I need a savior, I need improvement, I need you God,
I need the grace and mercy of the Lord
Ask the spirit to move in you and ye shall wait on the Lord
Lord order my footsteps and the words that come out of my mouth
Lord don't let my character be attacked; Lord continue in me with boldness and strength
Lord continue to shape and mold me
Let this day conform to your will and your word

Lord Let everything in me and of me be completed through your divine will with Love and according to your word. Help me to keep divine expectations. Keep me in your works; Let your will be done complete me Lord; with a spirit of forgiveness and pure love. Let the holy spirit stay within me always. Let me holdfast in faith and fear no one or anything but you Lord Jesus. Putting you first and let my body be dedicated to your will and let me pray an unselfish prayer, acceptable to you. Thank You Lord, now and forever - Amen

I have the peace of God

Lord I want more of you to experience the power of your resurrection in my life; Christ work in my life to help me defeat sin and live a new life. Let me become totally dependent of your atoning work on the cross. I want my work to be pleasing to you God. Thank You Lord, now and forever - Amen

I receive mercy

Lord strengthen me to help others to get to know you. If you see anything in me that is not pleasing to you Lord cleanse me. Lift me up through your Word Lord. I am grateful and thankful to you Lord.

Lord help me to detach myself from the ways of the wicked. Lord let me enjoy the work of my labour. Lord bless the work of my hands. Lord help me to stay focused on you and sharing the gospel. Lord you have my full attention. Help me to have a relationship with you Lord! Thank You Lord, now and forever - Amen

I am worthy

Lord help me to have righteousness through faith in Jesus Christ – the righteousness that comes from the God and not of self. Lord I want the power that comes from a spirit filled life. Lord help me grow in grace. Thank You Lord, now and forever – Amen

I have power

I must trust in you Lord; my faith and hope rest in you alone Lord, help me to have a real love for everyone because my soul wants to be cleansed from selfishness and hatred. As I have asked you to save me Lord and have trusted you to save me Lord I ask you to give me a pure heart to wholehearted love others warmly for I have a new life in you and you in me which will last forever Thank You Lord, now and forever – Amen

I have faith

Lord please show me the next steps that you have for me in my journey and let me discern your voice from deceit. Thank You Lord, now and forever – Amen

Lord give me abundant strength to be totally dependent on you. Continue to be my advocate. Lord help me to gain spiritual maturity. Thank you lord, now and forever – Amen

I ask and it is given

Lord don't let me look back at my old life with regrets or long for it again. Lord help me to let it go; so that it will not be able to hinder me again in moving forward. Help me to stay on the narrow path to eternal life. Lord continually work in my heart to not have me to give up on myself and help others. Thank you lord, now and forever -amen

I believe in doing good

Lord help me to be patient as you are patient with us. Lord don't let the past absorb my mind; Lord help me to suppress the negative memories. Thank You Lord, now and forever - Amen

Lord allow me to only want to accept your will and purpose for my life. Lord allow me to understand my purpose so that I don't abuse it. Lord help me to appreciate what you have given me. Thank You Lord, now and forever - Amen

I have a positive attitude

Lord I don't want to have false love for others. Lord help me with the battle of the flesh and the mind. Lord help me to be patient and know that you are not through with me yet. Lord help me to be able to understand me so that the spirit can deal with me. To your glory. Thank you lord, now and forever - Amen

I will not worry

Lord give me strength to go the extra mile and have the Hold Spirit lead and guide me. Thank you lord, now and forever - Amen

Lord allow the Holy Spirit to comfort and empower me. Lord help me to guard my hearing as the Holy Spirit dwells in it. Thank you lord, now and forever - Amen

I receive grace

Lord equip me to do the thing that you need me to do and what you have created me to do. Help me to help someone to be positively affected by my life and works. Lord allow me to be rooted and grounded in your work. Thank You Lord, now and forever – Amen

I believe in doing good

Lord allow me to decrease so that you can increase in my life; Lord let the Holy Spirit overcome the spirit overcome my flesh. Lord help me to be careful of what I say and do. Lord help me to change and understand when I am wrong and help me to make it right. Thank you lord, now and forever – Amen

I will not give up

Lord be my mediator. Help me to obey the leadership of the spirit and not to be overcome with evil; but let me overcome evil with good. Lord help me to not be entangled with bondage. Lord help me to be steadfast in your word. Thank you lord, now and forever – Amen

I have been redeemed

Lord have your Holy Spirit take over my conscience and don't let sin use me to operate in my spirit; Lord grant me wisdom that comes from Jesus.
Thank you Lord for forgiving me of all my sins past, present, and future. Thank you for ultimate sacrifice.
now and forever - Amen

I am grateful

God help me to control my tongue and not lie. Lord help me to turn from sins and from evil and do good. Lord help separate me from the world. Lord help me to be full of joy and prosperity. Lord allow me to operate the opposite of the world so that you can continue to work in me. Lord allow me to only operate in the spirit. Thank You Lord, now and forever – Amen

I am a protector

Lord help me to realize how blessed I am; no matter how things seem. Lord help me to give thanks in all things. Allow me to understand that current and past negative situations does not determine how blessed I am. Lord help to keep my life and my works in a position to be blessed. I am blessed and highly favored. I am blessed and there are benefits just because I am a child of God and the seed of Abraham's inheritance. Thank You Lord, now and forever - Amen

I am royalty

Lord help me to be fully and only dependent on you. Jesus, help me to humble myself with a strong desire and determination to obey you. Lord, help me to be done with excuses and take responsibility and accountability in parts in wrong doing. Thank you lord for healing and restoration. Thank you lord, now and forever - Amen

I am of a sound mind

Lord help me to have a mind set to do your work and dedicate my body back to you as a living sacrifice holy and dedicated to doing your work of winning souls. Lord, allow my mindset to stay on assembling in the house of the Lord. Thank You Lord, now and forever - Amen Transform my life Lord and come into me to be all you are. Lord allow me to see your glory and witness your power. Thank You Lord, now and forever - Amen

I trust in your word

Lord protect the anointing on my life from the Holy Spirit; Lord keep me empowered, hopeful, with unwavering faith and belief; Lord allow me to keep the word deep down in my heart. Thank you lord, now and forever - Amen

Lord allow me to not have a spirit of fear. Lord allow me to let go of the past and forgive and to have harmony and peace. Thank You Lord, now and forever - Amen

I believe in outreach

Verify your word in me Lord, Lord give me instructions so I can see what I need to do and turn my failures into success. Lord renew my mind and let me inherit your precious promises. Thank you lord, now and forever - Amen

Lord cover my home, my children, my family, my relationship with your precious blood; God shape my character and morals. Lord help me so you can train me up for your purpose. Thank you lord, now and forever - Amen

I am free from bondage

Heal me lord from all sin, transgression, sickness, anxiety, hatred Lord in my trials help me to be pleasant, strong and loving. So that you get the glory. Lord help me to fulfill your purpose in my life. Lord help me to grow and mature in your love and peace. To become deeply rooted in you and to stay focused on your kingdom agenda. Thank you lord, now and forever – Amen

I have authority

Lord help me to be kind and merciful and to take on your nature. Lord help me to break bad habits and to be strong while going through the process. Lord help me to break bad habits and to be strong while going through the process. Lord help me to get rid of making excuses. Help me to conclude that my actions and word are in line with your word. Lord, help me to keep a mindset to want to do better and to help others. Lord help me to follow after he who is perfect. Thank you lord, now and forever - Amen

I pray daily

Lord you have been good to me and I have been anointed by you grace and mercy. Lord I glorify you. Lord as you have promised please continue to protect me and be my provider. Thank you lord, now and forever – Amen

Lord keep me whole in my faithfulness, loyalty, dependability, timeliness, consistence, stability, works, tithing, worshipping, and wanting to do right. Thank you lord, now and forever – Amen

I am strong

Lord let me not be disappointed in any outcome or blame other people; cause you are in control of all things. Lord prepare me for when you come for me and to stand and do what I am supposed to do to receive my miracles. Thank You Lord, now and forever – Amen

I am kind

Lord let me have a forgiving, kind, patient spirit as you are to us. Lord shine through me and allow me to be obedient to you. I am a child of yours and you have given me the ability to receive all things. Lord help me to live by what I say. I believe and take hold of me Jesus and let me allow you to be all you want to be for me. Lord I receive deliverance. Thank you lord, now and forever - Amen

I have salvation

Lord keep my mind set on your leading and guidance Lord cause I depend on you. Thank You Lord, now and forever – Amen

Lord I want to change and live and do right let me delight myself in you. Thank You Lord, now and forever – Amen

Lord help me to keep a mind that is focused on you and to have a relationship with you that no one can break. Thank You Lord, now and forever – Amen

I am mighty

Lord allow your word to govern my life. I want to be dedicated and committed to the word and to be separated from the world and its evil influences. Lord keep me in your Word as it is necessary for holy living. Let my life be an example of your good and perfect works. Lord continue to transform me inside and out. Thank you lord, now and forever - Amen

I am just

Lord don't let my character and integrity be attacked continue to protect me, my mindset, my spiritual being and in loving others. Lord continue to help me grow in strength and boldness. Lord continue to make, shape, and mold me. Let my talents, uniqueness, and your will be manifested in your name and likeness. Call me to the role that you have ordered for me to full capacity, keep me on track as you have equipped me to complete the tasks that you have given me. Use me Lord and let your glory rest on my shoulders. Let me recognize my value and not think of myself more high that I ought to and understand that it is someone more important than me. Thank you lord, now and forever - Amen

I am enough

Lord let me receive your love, peace, and servant ship
Lord I need you in everything I do and go through. Thank You Lord, now and forever – Amen
Lord let me have a spirit of expectation and walk in to my purpose and fulfill your will for my life. Lord let me continue to trust in you and keep my eyes and focus on you. Lord lead and guide me. Thank You Lord, now and forever – Amen

I am love

Lord let me recognize who I can trust and who I can't and when I should speak and when I shouldn't. Lord let me forget the negative things and leave them behind me and humble myself before all people. Lord let me keep praising and honoring you. Thank you lord, now and forever - Amen

I am humble

Thank you Holy Spirit for leading and guiding me. Thank you for helping me with my daily problems and in my prayers. Thank you Lord for your grace. Thank you for forgiving me of my sins. Lord help me to have a positive attitude toward everything. Lord allow me to appreciate what grace has made available to me. Thank You Lord, now and forever - Amen

I have been forgiven

Lord I pray to always know that you have unconditional love for me, so I can have unconditional love for others. I also pray that I love them as you love me. To know and understand that your life was lived in love and that you left peace with us through the Holy Spirit. Through all the things of this world love and your word will be the only things that will remain throughout eternity. Thank You Lord, now and forever – Amen

I have joy

Lord show me my purpose and let it be fulfilled by your will. Lord allow me to have patience in all things to accept whatever I am going through and have your strength while I am going through it. To be a witness of your power, strength, and grace Lord everyday of my life. Thank you lord, now and forever - Amen

I am healed

Thank You Lord

Lord allow your angels to cover my comings and goings and to drive out the enemy of depression, sorrow, and sadness. Let my heart not be troubled or afraid. Lord eliminate the thoughts and time spent on the negatives and let me be excited and joyful for what you are doing in my life. Because it is good. Thank You Lord, now and forever – Amen

I am appreciative

Lord I pray for peace and serenity and the ability to smile and laugh cause the enemy will be defeated every time. Lord let me stay hungry and thirsty for your majestic power. A mind to assemble the more to come and hear your word and give thanks, glory, and praise to your name. A mind and heart to seek you ist, know you ist, come to you ist, communicate with you ist, honor you ist, love you ist, be obedient to you ist, give tithes and offerings to you ist, accept you and your word ist, praise you ist, pray to you ist, follow after you ist, and listen to you ist. And know that everything will fall into place and I will be able to see your glory, grace, mercy, righteousness, you love, your promises, and discern you from the enemy and be pleasing to you. Thank You Lord, now and forever - Amen

I have salvation

Lord increase my faith. Thank you for sending your word to me through true righteous people. Lord take these evil thoughts that I have no control over. Let me use all of this negative energy that I have used in the world to use to your likeness and to please you and to build your ministry. Let me and all of your people have an obedient mind unto you. Thank you lord, now and forever - Amen

I have been redeemed

Lord take my heart and my words as it is truly yours to be used to do your purpose in your kingdom with only the words you want me to say and tell the people that you want me to tell. Thank you Lord, now and forever - Amen

Lord let me have the mind that does not think or give care to what others think of me whether in church or in the world while I am praising you now and in the future. Thank You Lord, now and forever - Amen

I reign supreme over earthly sin

Lord let me know that I have been set free. Not bound by the chains of this world. To know that you have healed and delivered me to be right before you. Lord lay your hands on us in comfort and love. Let us walk in victory, knowing that we are already divinely blessed and spiritually blessed in heavenly places in Christ Jesus. Let us practice victory now with prosperity, health, success, protection, preservation of life, deliverance from the fear of death, triumph over deceit, defeated sin and the devil like Jesus did, success, understanding and wisdom.

We must ultimately believe, trust, and have faith in Jesus and the power of God. Thank You Lord, now and forever - Amen

I am watchful

Lord let me be able to help others, Lord let me have a renewed spiritual strength, long for righteousness, and present my body as a living sacrifice. Lord let me always enter into your gates with thanks and praise. A mindset to live upright and righteous and support Leadership for your purpose. Thank you lord, now and forever - Amen

I am hope

Lord allow me to stand firm and steadfast in prayer and believing; the shield of faith. Lord let me use my power and faith tools in my everyday life. Be clothed in it. Allowing you to work in me. Have a mind to submit, teach, show, guide and lead and be led by you and staying devoted to your word. Thank You Lord, now and forever - Amen

I am blessed

Lord allow your people to have wisdom and grace to make ends meet. To be honest in all things and keep us in your favor. Allow us to be born again and serve you. Let our measure of grace and faith be able to get us through our trials of life. Knowing that you are with us and never leaving us. Thank You Lord, now and forever – Amen

I am highly favored

Lord I thank you for your dreams and visions. Let me keep remembrance that I am more than a conqueror and that your joy is my strength. Lord allow your word to rule in my heart and draw nearer to you and let you have complete control over my life. To know everything is about you; for you to get the glory and that it is pleasing to you. Lord let me have the mind to worship, praise, and thank you each day.

Thank you lord, now and forever - Amen

I have abundant prosperity

Lord let me take your spirit with me wherever I go. Allow me to be watchful to the things I need to be and not to trust the things of this world. Lord let your will be done in my life. Lord I lean to you and your everlasting dominion which will not pass away or be destroyed. Lord allow me to meet the requirements of being faithful and abide in righteousness . Thank You Lord, now and forever - Amen

I have understanding

Lord allow me to possess the traits and characteristics of you and know that our routines and habits can be changed through belief in you
Thank you Lord
Pray to empty ourselves to meet the needs of people which are destined by God and by his will. After each prayer end with one of God's promises and allow yourself to
Give Thanks in all Things
praying for others is the act of unconditional love
We don't have to be perfect
when we go to the Lord
Pray for a spirit of wisdom and revelation through knowledge of him and everlasting life.
Thank you Lord

www.ingramcontent.com/pod-product-compliance
Lightning Source LLC
Chambersburg PA
CBHW070634050426
42450CB00011B/3194